Pangolin plays the mandolin

Lesley Sims

Illustrated by David Semple

The sun has set. The stars are out.
You cannot hear a thing...

Till Pangolin leaps out of bed
and **strums** her mandolin.

She plucks the strings.
She hums and sings.

She dances through the trees.

Tired Tiger starts to growl.
"What does she think she's doing?"

"We're trying to sleep," the monkeys howl.

Now Elephant is booing!

But Pangolin can't help herself.
Her mandolin is new.

She sings.

Tra la!

Tra lee!

Tra la!

She plays the whole night through.

At dawn, she yawns, climbs into bed...

A loud shout makes her jump.

HEY!

Pangolin can hardly sleep.

Her friends are cross all day.

That night, she has a bright idea.

I know just what to play!

At twilight, as the stars come out,
she strums a gentle tune.

"A lullaby," the monkeys sigh.
They sleep beneath the moon.

But oh dear me!
When morning comes,
her friends stay in their beds.

They've overslept.
They're fast asleep
and cuddling their teds.

So Pangolin sings loud and strong:

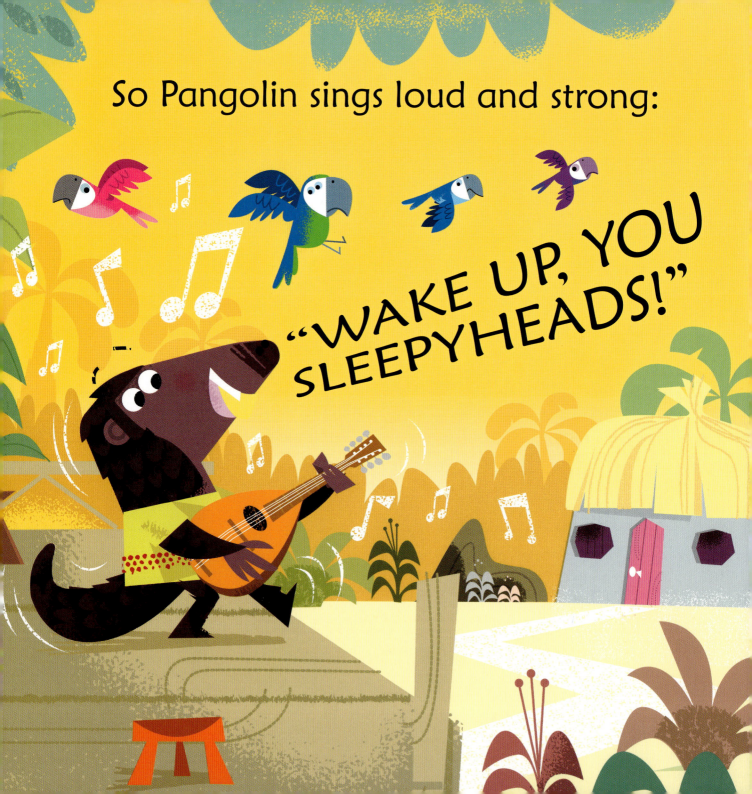

"WAKE UP, YOU SLEEPYHEADS!"

"What a great night's sleep I had!"
says Tiger, with a grin.

"And you're the best alarm clock, with your amazing mandolin!"

Starting to read

Even before children start to recognize words, they can learn about the pleasures of reading. Encouraging a love of stories and a joy in language is the best place to start.

About phonics

When children learn to read in school, they are often taught to recognize words through phonics. This teaches them to identify the sounds of letters that are then put together to make words. An important first step is for children to hear rhymes, which help them to listen out for the sounds in words.

You can find out more about phonics on the Usborne website at **usborne.com/Phonics**

Phonics Readers

These rhyming books provide the perfect combination of fun and phonics. They are lively and entertaining with great storylines and quirky illustrations. They have the added bonus of focusing on certain sounds so in this story your child will soon identify the short *a* sound, as in **pangolin** and **mandolin.** Look out, too, for rhymes such as **strings** – **sings** and **beds** – **teds**.

Reading with your child

If your child is reading a story to you, don't rush to correct mistakes, but be ready to prompt or guide if needed. Above all, give plenty of praise and encouragement.

Edited by Jenny Tyler
Designed by Sam Whibley

Reading consultants: Alison Kelly and Anne Washtell

First published in 2023 by Usborne Publishing Limited, 83-85 Saffron Hill, London EC1N 8RT, United Kingdom.
usborne.com Copyright © 2023 Usborne Publishing Limited. The name Usborne and the Balloon logo
are registered trade marks of Usborne Publishing Limited. All rights reserved. No part of this publication
may be reproduced, stored in a retrieval system, or transmitted in any form or by any means without
prior permission of the publisher. UE. First published in America in 2023.